Lexy and Bruce
the love letters

Jenny Mackay

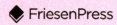 FriesenPress

Suite 300 - 990 Fort St
Victoria, BC, v8v 3K2
Canada

www.friesenpress.com

Copyright © 2021 by Jenny Mackay
First Edition — 2021

All rights reserved.

No part of this publication may be reproduced in any form, or by any means, electronic or mechanical, including photocopying, recording, or any information browsing, storage, or retrieval system, without permission in writing from FriesenPress.

ISBN
978-1-03-911078-6 (Hardcover)
978-1-03-911077-9 (Paperback)
978-1-03-911079-3 (eBook)

1. PETS, ESSAYS

Distributed to the trade by The Ingram Book Company

Table of Contents

Lexy and Bruce: The Love Letters   1

   Remembering the Day When We First Met   3

   The Washer   7

   Falling   11

   A Hospital Stay   15

   Our Beach Without You   19

   The Royal Treatment   23

   Remembering All Our Adventures   27

   Swimming Around the Issue   31

   Dear Momma   35

Lexy and Bruce: The Love Letters

a forever love...

Once upon a time, a senior pitbull named Lexy met a shark named Bruce. They loved each other dearly, and the relationship they shared can only be described as a fairytale.

Lexy was rescued at eight years young by beautiful humans as part of a cruelty investigation. She waited a very long time after that for a home, and once she found her forever family, the little lady felt safe, secure, and loved. Even with all of this, she felt an empty place in her heart. She needed a friend; she needed a *best* friend.

On a Tuesday afternoon many years ago, Lexy visited her local cookie store in hopes of finding a tasty treat. What she found was worth so much more. She peered to her left, she peered to her right, and what she saw directly in front of her was magical.

Lexy inched forward, twitching her nose, sniffing the air as she approached a shelf full of toys. She placed her paw on the edge, just a little past the middle, and slowly edged it forward through the soft and cozy plush, all the way back and deep into the shadows. Then, she pulled out a shark! This particular shark was a bit dusty and maybe his fins were a little crooked, but to Lexy, he was perfect. The shark smiled and lightly dipped his head in respect and thanks.

In that moment, they made a connection. They were both in need of so much, but especially of each other—a friend and family.

Lexy and her Bruce have been together ever since. They seize their moments and claim each one as a grand adventure. For, to them, simply being together is a privilege that makes the hearts of those around them skip a beat.

Their mutual gratitude for that chance meeting sometimes overwhelms them, and in response they exchange letters. They are love letters between best friends, a window into the purest of connections, and a love story for the ages.

#LexyAndBruceLoveLetters

Remembering the Day When We First Met

Dear Bruce,

Our first meeting wasn't that long ago, but I vividly remember our first glance. I felt a spark, and a kind of energy buzzed from the tip of my tail all the way to the tips of my paws.

　　Dare I say it was love at first sight? Maybe, but given my past, I only learned what love feels like when I met our Momma a few months ago. I am still trying to get used to it, and I hope the feeling is here to stay. Did you feel it too, Bruce?

On that day, I peered into your little shark eyes and recognized what I saw. It was the same look my eyes had when I was in the shelter. After months and months of being ignored, so many people came in to meet the animals in need and all of them just walked by my kennel, not a single one acknowledged me; not even a smile or a nod. They wanted puppies, dogs without a history. However, it was obvious that my body and I had a long story to tell. One day, all that changed. When I met Momma, she kneeled beside me told me I was perfect just the way I was.

So it was for me and Bruce when we first met. I recognized your perfection. In that cookie store, you were dusty and pushed so far to the back of the shelf. You were in the shadows, forgotten and alone. They had no idea how much you had to give. Your glorious sharky radiance brought light and blew the shadows away. I saw you clearly.

There and then, in that moment, I knew. I asked Momma if we could adopt you too, and later that night you and I were home, as family. I remember resting our heads and curling up together in front of the fire to dream. Our life together—our future—was in front of us.

As we begin our journey and write this fairytale that I know we will live, I am here to assure you, Bruce, that I will respect and love you till my last breath.

I can't wait to see what adventures await us!

You are forever my best friend.

Your Lexy, the pibble who loves you the most

Dear Lexy,

    Thank you very much for your letter. I have never received a letter before, so my little fins are clapping with glee; I can't seem to put it down. I've read it many times, folding and unfolding the pages, and I fear they may break apart, fall like snow, and blow away. Your words are special to me, so I hope you write to me again.

    In such little time, you have grown to know me so well, my Lexy. The first time we met, I knew we would be here in this moment. I too saw in your light—a heart, a love yearning to be fulfilled. Yes, I was dusty and overlooked, but maybe I was waiting for you. I hid till the time was right, and I knew I had found my "other."

I had never known love—not real love—until I met you. Periodically, humans would stop by my shelf in the cookie store and comment on how soft I was, but I was always "too big" or "too shark-like." I never understood what they meant.

They never saw that my love could be real and that by extension, I could be real (whatever "real" actually means). To me, it is not complicated: it is simply a state of being that elevates our emotions, our sense of self, and connection.

My little Lexy, you made me real.

I don't believe you saw a "toy shark"; I believe you saw hope. Hope for a future filled with possibility, friendship, shared secrets, and fun.

Lexy, the pibble who loves me the most, I can't wait to see what awaits us. My promise to you is that there will most definitely be adventure.

You are forever my best friend.

Your Bruce, the shark who loves you the most

The Washer

Dear Bruce,

    How are you? I am fine. Momma said the day had finally come, and that today would be the first day you visit the Washer; I don't know where that is, but it sounds scary. I hope you are okay. I admit that I haven't counted the minutes, but it feels like a number that couldn't possibly even be real. How could anyone count that high? You have been gone for such a very long time already. I miss you; please come home soon.

Without you by my side, I deeply feel the loss of adventure. So many things have happened already today, and I wish we had experienced them together. I can't wait to tell you about the day. I don't think I can even describe how I am feeling right now, bottling up all these moments till I see you. How long will that be? My inner self is bubbling over; I can't sit still, and my entire world is vibrating, buzzing with excitement and fear all at the same time. I miss you; please come home soon.

I've been walking around our home and talking to my toys, but none of them are you. I know they are trying to cheer me up, but their jokes only make me feel more lost without you, Bruce. You understand me so well, and you know exactly what tickles my funny bone!

You know how much I appreciate a tasty, delicate treat, but today my treats have lost their flavour. They don't even taste good.

And our favourite napping place in front of the fireplace? Well, it isn't warming me as it should, and it feels cold and lonely. I miss you Bruce. Please come home soon.

Even the beach feels since you left me. The sand between my paws only reminds me that I won't be bringing any of it home to remind you of the sea.

I watched our show on TV last night and laughed at the part, you know the one, where the cat... I can't even say it without laughing! Let's watch it together when you come home.

I miss you; please come home soon, Bruce. I'm not the same without you.

With love,

Your Lexy, the pibble who loves you the most

Dear Lexy,

    Thank you for your letter; it warmed my heart while I was away at the Washer. I miss you. I will be home very soon. I cannot wait to hear about your day and all the experiences you had. I am sorry that you felt a loss of adventure. I am a little ashamed to admit that while you were in need, I did have some amazing times! I am excited to share my new adventures with you. My fragile shark heart is in perpetual hope that you can forgive me. I promise, my Lexy, that my mind regularly turned to thoughts of you, wishing that you could take it in and feel all the moments too.

    At first, the Washer was a scary place. You are so clever to have guessed as much. You know me so well! It was cold and dark, and I couldn't see my fins in front of my eyes. Then, I looked up and our Momma opened the sky to bring so many of our friends to join me; the Crocodile was there, as was the Giraffe, and the Owl, and the Unicorn, too! Then, slowly at first, and soon much more quickly, the ocean poured in—and you know how much I love the ocean! Finally, all our friends and I were swimming with glee. The ocean started to spin and spin, and we all rode the waves, tossing and turning, to and fro, for quite some time. We bounced around, laughing as mysterious, soapy bubbles floated and popped above our heads.

After what felt like seconds (but I know it was much longer), the soapy bubbles dissolved, and the ocean drained away. Soon, our friends and I were whisked away to a warm place where we danced on the wind until our insides and our outsides were toasty and dry. I wish I knew where this place was and how to find it again. Other than being next to your side in front of our fireplace, this is the coziest I have ever felt.

Momma told me that only plushies like me can visit the Washer. This is my greatest sorrow, because it was so much fun, and I know you would enjoy it too. Oh well, we have many other adventures ahead of us to share. So, my Lexy, let's make them count!

I am excited to come home soon. And I should apologize. I do smell a bit funny now—kind of like the flowers you like to pee on in our backyard.

I hope you recognize me... I will be the shark who loves you the most.

With love,

Your Bruce

Falling

Dear Bruce,

I needed a little time to collect my thoughts about the accident. Until now, I didn't feel able to speak from my heart. In that moment when Momma leaned over to take a photo of us, I was fast asleep, and it startled me, Bruce. I jumped, and before I knew it, you were travelling all the long way down, twirling in the wind for what felt like minutes in slow motion until you landed on the cold floor.

It has been two days since that horrible night when I accidentally pushed you off the soft, cozy tower. It's so high up—higher than anything I've ever seen! I need to climb my steps to get there and, of course, you know I always carry you too so we can enjoy the view together. I feel so sorry for what I did.

Momma said you fell to the hardwood. I don't really know what that is, but I know it's bad. I saw you falling and falling, fin over fin. Every once in a while, I spied your eyes, wide open, looking afraid and right back into mine. These moments lasted forever and tore into my heart, where these images will live forever. Then, I heard a terrible sound and saw you there. You dented your nose, and your little fin was even more crooked than when we first met.

I cried a lot, but Momma said that she could mend you and that she could straighten your fin, but your nose may always be dented. Momma assured me that this means that I would always be able to recognize you, even in a sea full of sharks. She promised that you'd be better than new soon, but I need to be very gentle with you for a while. I promise to be quiet and nap close to you every day.

I know I should only think about how I can take care of you and the adventures we will have soon. But that's pretty tough to do. I know that over time, this too shall pass, but maybe I need a few more days to mourn your pain.

With love,

Your Lexy, the pibble who loves you the most

P.S.: Please excuse the blotchy spots on your letter. I was checking to ensure that all my feelings were clear, that what I wrote captured my heart, and forgot that I was crying.

Dear Lexy,

    Thank you very much for your letter. I am so grateful for all the love you show me, all the love we share, and this new letter. Your letters make me feel important. It is an honour to feel so real. I know that what happened was an accident, and my shark eyes are crying the ocean, knowing how sad you feel.

    When I was falling from the cozy tower, I saw you—I caught glimpses of your face and your eyes as I tumbled through the air for what felt like hours. I know we both felt so very scared. But, like one of our adventures, we experienced it together. There is nothing you and I can't overcome when we face it together.

You are so right to say that the tower is very high up. It must be at least fifteen fins high! When I fell, my life flashed in my mind, and you know what I saw? It was only you and the many moments we spent together! I remembered the time we went to Times Square and when we ran up the Rocky steps in Philadelphia. I remembered all our matching outfits and our Christmas Day beach ritual. Every single Christmas, we go to the beach and play in the sand and snow, it is one of the beautiful moments I look forward to the most because it's purely ours. Yes, Momma is there too, but only we know that for us, this outing symbolizes the closure of one chapter and the glorious welcome of the next. Most pitbulls and sharks celebrate the New Year, but you and me, my Lexy who loves me the most, we prance to our own dream schedule!

Most of all, I remembered the day we first met, the day you chose me from the cookie store shelf and gave me a forever home.

Accidents happen, but our friendship is not one of them. We were meant to be together.

Yes, after the fall, my nose is dented, and we know that my fin will never be perfectly straight, but it's just more evidence of my Velveteen Shark status... Your love made me real.

I am excited for our next adventure... And I am excited to just nap beside you.

With love,

Your Bruce, the shark who loves you the most

A Hospital Stay

Dear Lexy,

Momma told me you were not feeling well and had to spend the weekend at the hospital. I went to bed and you were cuddled beside me; when I woke up, you were nowhere to be found. I looked in front of the fireplace, I looked in the sunny spot in the backyard... I even looked for you among the pile of neatly folded blankets because I know you like to play pranks with Momma and mess them all up. I couldn't find you, and I was afraid.

Momma comforted me and told me all about the hospital. She said it's a place you go to feel better. She said that you needed fluids. Because my shark eyes were already leaking the ocean, I offered you mine, but Momma said that you needed something different. I am so sorry that I couldn't help you, my Lexy. I am missing you so much. I am sad you had to go away, but I am glad that you are with people who will make you feel better so you can come home to me.

While you have been gone, I've been watching over all the other toys. The Unicorn and Owl were particularly concerned for you. I told them bedtime stories about adventures we've had, but these were so grand that the plan backfired, and most of the toys stayed up all night asking questions about the world outside. I promised them that one day, we would all take an adventure together. When you get home, let's talk about where we should take our little crew and what we should all do.

I told the toys about our road trip to California and the time we flew on a plane to New York City. We sure learned to know and love hotel living and all the perks of travel food! I think the drive-thru is my new favourite adventure. YUM! I told them about the time you sacrificed yourself to protect me from a raccoon and that time when you stole three pounds of cheese and buried it in the sofa cushions. Do you remember how hard we laughed when Momma sat on it? She was so startled! Silly momma! I also told them about the first time we met and how it changed my life for the better—forever!

All these happy memories helped with the pain of missing you.

Momma said you should be well enough to come home late tomorrow night. I am writing you this letter because I miss you so much, and I want you to know that I am waiting for you.

I couldn't wait or tell you personally. I was afraid that my shark eyes would start to leak the ocean, and I don't want to make you feel sad.

When you come home, let's be still together, stay up late, and whisper about all our adventures yet to come.

Forever.

Your Bruce, the Shark who loves you the most

Dear Bruce,

Momma came to visit me at the hospital today, and she brought your letter. I was still a little drowsy, but I honestly could not wait to hear what you wrote, so I asked her to read it to me there and then.

Your words brought a tear to my eye and made my heart feel so warm and fuzzy. I felt your pain in that letter, and I know you are missing me as much as I am missing you. Remembering all our adventures healed me as much as the hospital did. You are my most favourite and special little Nurse Shark.

But my Bruce, I cannot lie to you, so I must admit that I was so afraid of not knowing what would happen next. After Momma left, I was all alone in my room until the Doctor's arrived. During that time, your words helped me remember that I had so much to fight for.

Through thick and fin, we have been there for each other for years now—no battle too tough, no roadblock too high. Bruce, you are my inspiration to achieve so much more than I ever thought I could.

I remember the first time we met—my gosh, was that six years ago now? I saw you on the shelf of our local cookie store and knew instantly that we were meant for each other. You were the only shark in the store—dusty from waiting so long for a home and lonely, being the only of your kind. I recognized in you the same feelings I had before Momma brought me home. You were so precious, a true gentleshark, and you allowed me to come to you and didn't ask anything from me except respect and kindness. I will never understand how you were overlooked by so many. You were such a beautiful soul in need of love, friendship, and the space to breathe and become your purest self. I don't even think you needed any time to understand me either, for our connection was most definitely immediate and strong.

I remember that first night at home together as if it were yesterday. I carried you over the threshold, and our partnership was complete. Within minutes, we were snoozing together in front of a roaring fire. Who knew that meeting your soulmate is such exhausting work?

Of all my life Bruce, my proudest and most profound moment is the time I chose you and you chose me.

Thank you for loving me unconditionally and unselfishly, and for being my very best friend forever.

Your Lexy, the pibble who loves you the most

Our Beach Without You

Dear Bruce,

    I went to our beach without you today, and I feel a heavy sense of guilt because I know this is our special place; we have enjoyed so many beautiful days there swimming, building sandcastles, and watching sunsets while we strolled along the promenade.

    I hope no one reached out to tell you about before this letter gets to you and that you have time to read it. I needed you to hear it from me. I needed to tell you myself about my trip and explain why.

There is no easy way to tell you this, my Bruce. When I was recently at the hospital, the Doctor was very kind to me, and she took lots of tests. But sadly, she told me these tests revealed that I have cancer. I have been here before; do you remember a few years ago when I had surgery to remove a lump on my leg? I have been cancer-free for three years, but it is back and much more serious than before. I am strong, and I will fight this with all I have because I need more time with you. The Doctor said I may need two surgeries followed up by chemotherapy and recommended that I start treatment immediately. Throughout this process, whenever I am afraid, I will think of you. Whenever I feel that maybe I can't beat this, I will think of how loved you make me feel. Whenever I feel tired, I will let my mind drift away into a beautiful dream about our adventures, past and future.

How are you, Bruce? I know this is a lot to take in, and I can only hope that you understand how much I worry about how deeply this will affect you. This is life. Sometimes it gives us everything we could want, like a best friend like you, and at other times, we must deal with things that are hard or unimaginable—the things we would never want. I will be right here beside you every step of the way. We will have to work together to keep each other strong. I don't know what awaits me on the other side of the treatments but hear this now, Bruce: I will not count the minutes with you. I will not belittle everything we have by allowing that. I will count the number of times my heart skips a beat when we go on an adventure and the many ways you show me how much you care, even before breakfast. My only concern is that maybe I can't count that high, so let's just agree now that the number in infinite.

I am so sorry for keeping my diagnosis a secret from you for all these weeks. I wanted to enjoy some time with you, untainted by your knowing what I was going through and the possibility that one day I may need to leave you. I hope that you can understand, that you can forgive me and still see me as you did before you heard this news.

With love,

Your Lexy, the pibble who loves you the most

Dear Lexy,

    Recently, you wrote me a letter apologizing for going to the beach without me; I understand that you needed space to think. When you are hurting, I only tell you how much I love and respect you. That is true for every part of you, including the decisions you make.

    When we are apart, I am keenly aware of our forever friendship. Best Friend status is not something I take lightly. This is precisely why your news was so incredibly beyond sad to hear. Yes, I know I need to focus on the here and now, to see you as if nothing has changed, but my Lexy, so much is now changed. Our future and our present will take a new and unforeseen direction.

My little shark heart is shattering while I write this, but I am confident that the next time I see you, just one look at your beautiful soul will cure me. You are my true north, and I am your true south; our oneness is magnetic, and it will make us forever one.

From the day we met in the cookie store, I knew you chose me. You did not choose the shark on the left or the shark with bright colours. I was dusty and hidden away, but you found me. You rescued me. You chose me because I was right for you.

It's okay for you to keep some thoughts just for you. I don't see them as secrets. Rather, I see them as your holding onto things that you'd rather show me than tell me. And you always show me; at this point, my Lexy, I know you with all my heart. Whether you know it or not, you always show me.

You are so brave for fighting cancer with all you have, but I also want you to know that I don't want you to suffer for me. I can't imagine being without you, but I also can't stomach the idea of your being in pain or silently suffering. Strength is admirable, but it can also be a weakness, and it can hold us back from the truth.

To me, my Lexy, you are practically perfect and a little magical in every way.

With love,

Your Bruce, the shark who loves you the most, with all his heart and soul

The Royal Treatment

Dear Bruce,

I feel your support and know you stand beside me, always. This doesn't make it any easier to discuss my cancer diagnosis with you, because I am keenly aware of how much it pains you.

As you know, I started chemotherapy five months ago. My gosh, the oncologist's office is so very far away. Momma said it's because the Doctor is the best, but I think she secretly picked it so I would get a nice car ride out of it. Momma is thoughtful that way, like when she pretends to be too full at dinner to finish her plate and gives me her leftovers. Have you ever noticed these are always the foods I love the most?

These past months, my treatments have been going well. After each one, I felt like I could conquer the world. I was energized and found my inner puppy. After each session, Momma and I went to the cookie store and she let me pick any treat I wanted. Have I ever told you that, Bruce? And guess what cookie store we go to—the very same place we first me all those years ago, Bruce. I guess I received two treats with each visit.

Today I had a chemotherapy session that did not go so well. I know I told you this morning when we said goodbye that I would be home soon. I think it may take me a bit longer.

After my chemotherapy, Momma and I were on the way home when I started to feel unwell. We drove to the Animal Emergency Hospital. This is where I am now and where I need to stay for a few days.

Please don't worry, Bruce. Everyone here is showing me love and attending to my every need. They are treating me like a queen. I know you so well, Bruce, I know that as you read this, you are trying to figure out how you can get here to be by my side. For now, I need you to be strong. I need you to be my king and protect our kingdom. Will you please look after the toys, guard our special place in front of the fire, and give Momma a kiss from me when she arrives home and gives you this letter?

Momma needs us both so much right now.

The Doctor says my white blood cell count and heart rate are far too high, and my temperature is far too low. I am cozily wrapped in a special warming blanket. They think this is likely related to chemotherapy. Momma said she knew that the treatment posed a risk and didn't want to put me through this again, and she needed to take time to think about whether to continue. Maybe, Bruce, you could take her to Our Beach. It is a very good place to sit, think, clear your mind, and focus.

Please, don't worry.

To my Bruce, the Shark who loves me the most, today is a blip in our world. I will be home with you in just two sleeps.

With love,

Your Lexy, the pibble, who loves you the most

Dear Lexy,

    The honours you bestow on me are too many. Everything tells me that I would be better suited as your faithful, fearless knight fighting for you, rather than a king to stand beside you. But of course, my Lexy, I will forever do as you wish.

    Momma brought me your letter, and I gave her a kiss just like you asked.

    We have been best friends for seven years, Lexy, and I wish I could understand how, after all this time, my heart starts to beat so very fast every time I see your paw-writing on the envelopes that deliver such beautiful feelings through your letters. I hope that you truly understand how magical you are and how amazing you make those around you feel. Quite simply, you make this world a better place simply for being in it.

    It makes my shark heart happy to know that Momma still takes you to our cookie store. I will never forget that moment we met for as long as I live—and forever beyond that, too.

When Momma got home and gave me your letter, she asked me to sit with her before I read it. I have never seen Momma look so serious with clouds in her eyes.

She talked about our first meeting and how it was like the sunrise in both of our personalities and our beautiful life together. Momma told me that I need to start to prepare for our inevitable sunset.

Momma explained about your chemotherapy. I wished that I could have endured it for you, but I know that's not how it works. So, now I only wish that I could be with you, my fin holding your paw. Momma told me, Lexy, that you are tired and need rest. If I promised to be a very quiet shark, I wonder if your doctors would let me come to your side.

Momma explained that you were slowing down; those clouds in her eyes started to rain while she told me just how sick you are. She said it is her job, and it is my job too, to make you feel comfortable. It is our job to listen to you closely and respect your wishes when you tell us your body is just too tired and needs to sleep forever.

Momma confirmed that there would be no more chemotherapy for you. She said this is not giving up—instead, it is giving you everything.

From this day forward, every day we spend together will be an adventure of epic scale. Let's show Momma we are not afraid of anything because we are together.

You will be away for two more sleeps, Lexy. When you are better, let's get away and take a trip. I will pack your bags, tiaras, tutus, hoodies, and maybe a fancy dress too, because you never know where adventure will lead.

Let's get away, little Lexy. Let's make new friends and leave those we meet in a sea of wonder at all that is possible when you believe.

With love,

Your Bruce, the shark who loves you the most

REMEMBERING ALL OUR ADVENTURES

Dear Bruce,

It is so amazing to believe that yet another year has passed. Another snowfall, another birth of spring, another sunny summer at the beach, and another autumn crunching through the leaves.

All of this has me reflecting on the amazing life we have shared so far. What adventures we have enjoyed! Is there anything that we haven't experienced yet?

Our first real adventure was conquering the ocean. I was so afraid to dip my toes in, but I heard your voice encouraging me. The promise of you teaching me the shark-fin-flop motivated me to be brave. Why? Because I wanted to experience your world, Bruce. I wanted to feel your sense of freedom.

Since then, our life together has been a blur with adventure after adventure.

You and Momma surprised me with a birthday cake every year. Every single Christmas, we went to the Beach.

Together, we raised money for dog rescues and shark conservation—a way to honour us both. We raised funds and awareness for Pet Food Banks and Animal Blood Banks.

We made new friends and were featured is many books. We even had our own calendar!

We travelled a lot, too. Can you believe we flew on a plane to New York and Hollywood? We drove in a car to Philadelphia and took a road trip all the way through Washington State, Oregon, and California. We spoke at a conference in Anaheim and stopped to visit new friends in Southern California and Seattle.

We ran up the Rocky steps.

We took a road trip close to home, too; we spent a week travelling through Vancouver Island, BC. We spent a lazy afternoon touring the waterways on a canoe and a kayak. We visited our capital city, the parliament buildings, and a farm. We saw goats on a roof eating grass and walked on miles and miles of sandy beaches.

But the very best, through all our years of adventures so far, is that we ate so much ice cream!

Thank you, Bruce, my friend, confidant, and accomplice for giving me the courage to experience this world and to be free as I savoured every moment.

With love,

Your Lexy, the pibble who loves you the most

Dear Lexy,

    Thank you very much for your letter and for reminding me of the moments we have shared. The memories are always with me, but the finer details are what define the moments that take your breath away.

    I love that you pay attention to the changing of a season. You are so attentive to the world in which we live. For my part, Lexy, I have seen only the passage from night to day, as it is the day where our adventures begin. We have had so many adventures, but I hope you can excuse me if I say that my greatest adventure is simply being by your side wherever, whenever, and however you wish me to be. This is not to say that I live for you, but rather that our lives are so intertwined that my peace is found in your peace.

With all the flotsam and jetsam floating around in this world, it is comforting to have our memories and trinkets firmly rooted for us, to visit how we please.

Tradition is important. This year let's make your birthday cake even bigger, with a layer for every one of your years. Let's swim and test your shark-fin-flop on Christmas Day!

I was—am—so honoured to lend my fin to support dog rescue, and I feel so blessed that you wanted to bring attention to my family, too. My shark eyes leaked the ocean when you, my Lexy, raised awareness about the tragedy of shark finning.

I was so shy at our first photoshoot. Like our Momma, I am a bit of an intro-shark—not like you, Lexy, my little extra-pibble who craves the friendship of all you meet. You amaze me. How is it that you came from such a tragic past but hold no grudges, hesitance, or fear?

True superheroes don't wear capes; they demonstrate forgiveness the way you do.

Whether it's on a boat, a plane, a car, or a walk... Wherever you are, I will be there with you.

Lexy, I am honoured to be your shadow, to be beside you, to protect you, and to adventure on forever with you.

I am blessed to be an equal partner in this most amazing time in our lives, as well as in our friendship, which will live on for the ages.

With love,

Your Bruce, the shark who loves you the most

Swimming Around the Issue

Dear Bruce,

    We have been swimming around this issue for months now, but I want you to know I have made my peace with it. I do not even consider it day to day; it exists but does not define me.

    Yes, one day, we don't know when, but there will be a day when this disease—when cancer—will take me from you. But let's take comfort that it will not be today.

    Today, let's just treasure the time we have. Let's go back to living in the moment, experiencing every adventure and feeling as if it were the first time for both of us.

Let's go back to what it all meant when we did not have a care in the world because, my Bruce, the only care I have now is spending moments with you: sharing secrets and staying up late watching scary movies. (I so appreciate that you put your fin over my eyes to save me from the really scary bits!)

I am so grateful, Bruce, that you and Momma will have each other forever. It is that thought and assurance that gives me the peace and strength that I need.

I am not in pain. But recently you asked me what I felt in my heart. I am compelled to focus on my life as a whole, not just a moment of my journey.

As you will remember, for the first eight years of my life, I was in pain. I was neglected and abused; my body hurt from lack of food and my soul was hungry for love.

All of this was caused by human greed. So many of my babies were sold for profit; I wonder if they ever think about the mother who let them go. I didn't have a choice.

Then, one day, beautiful humans saved me. They drove me miles and miles away, and they healed my body and most of my heart.

For many months I waited for my forever home. I waited for anyone to notice me.

I met Momma, and my heart started to heal again. I finally knew love and security.

And then, Bruce... I met you. My heart not only healed, but it *grew*. Sometimes, I feel like it will burst through my chest because of how you make me feel.

With you, I am stronger. I am brave; I am not afraid of living for today.

In closing, my Bruce, you make my life whole and give me purpose.

Your happiness drives me.

Please never forget that.

With love,

Your Lexy, the pibble who loves you the most

Dear Lexy,

    Your last letter stopped my heart. My gills closed and for a moment, and I felt myself falling, gliding like a leaf in the wind, silently into the abyss.

    I saw your face in my mind; your eyes were telling me that you needed me now more than ever. Without your eyes showing me, I could have let myself continue to fall and fall, eventually gently finding myself on the sandy ocean floor.

    But I am here with you, Lexy, as I always have been and always will be.

I know, Lexy, that you say that you have made your peace with your cancer diagnosis. But I have not.

My strength is not endless like yours. I am still trying to catch up. I feel like I am swimming against the current.

But knowing that I am swimming to be with you... Well, this is my food and my air. You are my ocean.

Lexy, you are forever my true north, and you will always be my home.

I will keep trying to get to where you are—to acceptance of the present, without sadness, resentment, guilt, or fear.

Today, being with you, near you, for you... This is my utopia and highest truth.

My Lexy, you give me courage to be pure, honest, and transparently weak.

When you leave, my little shark eyes will leak the ocean. But my Lexy—the pibble who loves me the most—the memories we made and are making... These will be the legacy we share, and they represent the purpose of my life.

My life, my love, my memories all started the day we first met, and I thank you for accepting me just as I am—flaws, fins, and all.

It doesn't matter how much longer we have together because "forever" lives in the heart.

With love,

Your Bruce, the shark who loves you the most

Dear Momma

It has been one month since Bruce and I left you.

Seven hundred and forty-four hours; forty-four thousand six hundred and forty minutes. It sounds like a very long time, no matter how you count it. And Momma, it does in fact feel like eternity already.

We have acutely felt this passage of time, knowing that we have each other while you are at home missing the shark and the pibble who will forever love you the most.

I want you to know that you made our last day so overwhelmingly beautiful. It is important you know that you made every single day feel like a dream.

On our last day, Bruce and I felt so free sitting in the front seat, driving through the park in that flashy red convertible. And it was the first time I ever had a cheeseburger and fries; it made me giggle,

Momma, that you let me have that for breakfast! We even stopped at the cookie store, and you let me pick out any fancy treat I wanted—not just one, but *three*! After a lazy morning sleeping in late, it sure did turn out to be a fun-filled, yummy day!

I felt your hesitation during our very last car ride, Momma, but I need you to know that you made the right decision for me. Then, when I was lying on top of that sea of cozy blankets with Bruce by my side, I need you to know that I heard every word you said. Bruce and I both felt every word. I heard every breath you took and felt every breath you missed while you sobbed.

Bruce and I thank you for your respect in acknowledging our need to move on together. You didn't hesitate. You didn't even second-guess. With the kindness you always show us, your voice was resolute in declaring that "Lexy and Bruce must be together forever." We thank you for making everything feel comfortable, for ensuring I was warm and wearing my favourite jammies with the butterfly print, for bringing my cozy blanket, and placing Bruce under my paw.

Bruce and I stayed with you after for as long as we could. We listened to all the stories you shared out loud about our life together. It made my heart feel so good hearing and seeing you smile and even laugh a little through all your tears.

Slowly, everything started to look a little fuzzy and that room drifted away. Bruce and I held each other close, and you will never believe what happened next, Momma! Our eyes suddenly refocused, and what we saw was magical.

My Bruce and I found ourselves at our beach. The sun was high in the sky, shining brightly down on us. All of Bruce's dents and patchy plush were undented and new. His squeaker regained its full squeak. I think that in that moment, Momma, Bruce really and truly did become real. And me! I could run fast and jump so high. My little pibble hips and knees were brand new. My frosted, silver face was a little less frosted.

Bruce and I are together, exactly as we were when we first met. The clock reset to our most blessed moment.

We have been spending all our time at our beach, playing in the waves, digging in the sand, finding all the good smells to roll in, and gnawing on barnacles that stick to the rocks at low tide.

We often stop at food trucks on the boardwalk for treats. Do you remember, Momma, how we used to do that at our beach? I know you enjoyed buying me ice cream just as much as I always enjoyed eating it. There is ice cream where I am now, Momma. I thought you'd like to know that.

Please don't be sad, Momma.

I know you miss Bruce and me, but we are free, safe, and together. We will be with you forever, in your memories and in your heart.

The next time you see me in your dreams, please know that it is real. There will be times when you wake from a sleep because you feel a nudge in the place next to you where I used to sleep. Don't doubt yourself, Momma, please know that it is real, and I am with you.

Be safe, Momma. Be well. Know that I think of you every day, and I pray that you can love again soon.

Forever your Lexy and your Bruce,

Your family who will forever love you the most.

Lexy and Bruce
A love story for the ages

About the Author

Jenny Mackay started working on *Lexy and Bruce: The Love Letters* through a creative writing course with the University of British Columbia's Extended Learning program. Soon, this informal project became a way to deepen her family connection and give a voice to Lexy and Bruce's special bond.

    Jenny lives in Vancouver, BC, with her partner, Mike. Their home is in the West End of the city, just two blocks from the beach where Lexy and Bruce had some of their favourite adventures. After losing Lexy to cancer in 2020, Jenny and Mike were able to open their hearts to another senior rescue pitbull named Caper.

CPSIA information can be obtained
at www.ICGtesting.com
Printed in the USA
BVHW051339031021
617774BV00012BA/486